Happy 5th Birthday
Nicki

Love
Andy and
Josi

Happy 5th Birthday

THE WILDLIFE OF
CANADA

Featuring the photography of Tom W. Hall

Text and captions by David Black

Designer
Philip Clucas MSIAD

Production Director
Gerald Hughes

Commissioning Editor
Trevor Hall

Editorial Director
David Gibbon

Publishing Director
Ted Smart

CLB 1847
Published 1987 by Bramley Books
Copyright © 1987 Colour Library Books Ltd.,
   Guildford, Surrey, England.
Printed and bound in Hong Kong by Lee Fung ASCO.
ISBN 0 86283 522 4

BRAMLEY BOOKS

THE WILDLIFE OF
CANADA

Featuring the photography of
Tom W. Hall

Text by
David Black

BRAMLEY BOOKS

In terms of its landscape, Canada is a young country. Its natural regions assumed their present form as recently as 10,000 years ago. It was then that the Ice Age waned and the climate warmed, allowing plants to invade from the south and west, thus setting the stage for the invasion of animal life. The influx of animal life came across the Bering land bridge and also from the south, the new arrivals mingling with the animals that had evolved on the North American continent itself, of which the pronghorn antelope is probably the best example.

It is from the south, though, that the region is enriched today during the summer months when hundreds of species of birds visit Canada to breed – the waders and wildfowl to the Arctic tundra and the warblers, those small and animated songsters, to the forested regions. There is even great migratory movement among the resident animals, such as the treks of the caribou as they move north from their sheltered, forested wintering grounds to the tundra to breed. Because the winters are so harsh, the animals that do not migrate have evolved ingenious methods of survival both under the snow and on top of it. Hunters and hunted may sport white-coloured coats in a critical survival game of hide and seek.

Canada has five main natural regions. The Arctic, the largest in area, includes the Arctic Ocean itself, large and numerous islands, pack ice and ice floes and, to the south, the treeless tundra. South of this region, extending in a great arc, is the coniferous or northern forest, similar to the great taiga of the Soviet Union. The prairie provinces of Alberta, Saskatchewan and Manitoba are named for the grasslands that extend northwards from the United States, bordered for the most part by aspen parkland. The Western Cordillera mountain range and Pacific Coast make up the fourth distinctive region and one particularly rich in wildlife, while the fifth region consists of the mixed hardwood forests of Ontario and the Maritimes.

Despite these distinct regions, there is often a great merging of one into another, while within each region there are, owing to the climate and local topography, great differences in vegetation and animal life.

The Far North

Covering a vast 2,500,000 square miles, the Canadian Arctic is described as a cold desert. But this belies the beauty of the place, with its varied ice forms, icebergs and glaciers, the sculptured tundra landscape with mounds and craters and geometric fractures known as polygons. Long lines of open water known as leads allow whales to travel round the pack ice, while polynias, roundish areas of open water created by currents, provide oases for wildlife just as waterholes do in the arid deserts of the South.

For a few intense summer months the Arctic is transformed into a breathtaking mixture of colored shrubs, flowers and lichens. Attracted by the rich insect and marine life come the breeding birds, the subtle shaded sandpipers, clamorous geese and majestic swans. Following on come the ravens and skuas, professional thieves of eggs and young.

The most famous animal of the region is the polar bear, a powerful animal that can measure up to 11 feet (3.4m) in length and weigh up to 1,200 pounds (540kg). This cunning hunter is forever sniffing the air for prey, particularly seals. In the early spring it seeks out newly-born ringed seals in their snow caves. Once one of these is detected, the bear pounds it open with its massive forepaws backed up by its tremendous bulk. At other times of the year adult seals are taken at their breathing holes. But the polar bear will take anything it can, from eider ducks grabbed underwater to young walrus on the edge of ice floes.

Apart from the polar bear, many other animals sport white winter coats. The Arctic fox has a thick, long-haired coat and a large, bushy tail which it uses to cover itself when sleeping. The Arctic fox is a common animal on the pack ice, following polar bears and feeding off the remains of their kill. The ptarmigan assumes a white plumage during the winter, when it shelters in snow drifts to avoid the icy winds. Ptarmigan are unique among chicken-like birds in having feathered toes, which help them walk on loose snow. The ptarmigan's main enemy is the goshawk, the largest of the falcons, with its black-spotted white plumage. Another avian predator of these parts, the snowy owl, subsists mainly on lemmings, small rodents famous for their mass movements when numbers outstrip the food supply.

The sociable harp seal spends the summer months in Arctic waters, but in the autumn journeys south to whelp in early spring on the ice in the gulf and off Newfoundland shores. As many as two million animals join in this migration, and on their breeding grounds there may be as many as six thousand animals to one square mile of pack ice. Since 1750 the harp seal has formed the basis of the Newfoundland sealing industry, and, although the animal is not endangered, every year the kill promotes an international outcry from the conservation fraternity. The young seals, or "whitecoats," are killed mainly for their fur, skin and oil. What is amazing is that the young seals are nursed for just two weeks, and during that time grow enormously fat – up to 110 pounds (45kg). Less well known outside Canada is the fact that other seals are hunted at this time, notably the young "bluebacks" of the hooded seal. Unlike true seals, male hooded seals have a large, elastic nose cavity that when inflated looks like a black rubber football.

The barren ground caribou is an animal that links the Arctic tundra with the evergreen forests to the south. In spring it leaves the forests on a trek several hundred miles to the north, where the calves are born on windswept uplands. Caribou tend to follow the same path each year, following frozen lakes and eskers - long, narrow hills of soil and rock dumped by glaciers. The pregnant cows lead the herd, followed by the juveniles and the bulls, who tend to lag further and further behind. The caribou's traditional enemy is the wolf, which may take up to 14 caribou each year. Hunting in packs, wolves chase the caribou in relays, or ambush them along their well-worn trails. By taking mainly sick and old caribou, wolves maintain a healthy breeding stock. The hooves of caribou splay widely to support the animal in snow and on swampy ground. They also function as strong paddles when swimming and as scoops when the animal has to scrape away the snow in winter to get at its staple winter diet of lichens. Micmac Indians named the caribou *xalibu*, meaning the one who paws, and it is probably from this name that the present one has been derived.

Evergreen Forest
The whole central part of the Canadian Shield plateau is made up of dense stands of coniferous forest interspersed with swampy muskeg, which covers more than a quarter of the country. Seemingly endless in extent, it is limited in composition to relatively few species of trees. Fir, spruce, pine and tamarock are dominant, with deciduous "weed trees" such as poplar and willow fringing the streams and rivers. It is here that is found one of Canada's most famous animals, the beaver, a remarkable animal whose engineering works have a profound effect on the landscape. By damming up streams the flow of water is stabilized, and at the same time pools are created that encourage wildlife such as trout to linger in the sheltered waters. The beaver's main objective in damming the streams is to create ponds deep enough that they do not freeze up in winter, thus providing deep-water storage beneath the ice for their winter food supply of sticks and twigs. Their famous lodges, about 15 feet (4.5m) across, are built of intertangled sticks plastered together with mud, which freezes hard to a concrete-like consistency, making the lodge predator proof. Each lodge has two underwater openings, for exit and entry. The beaver's tail is a versatile organ. It serves both as a rudder and paddle when swimming, and a balancing organ when hauling wood overland. When danger threatens, the beaver smacks its tail hard against the water, producing a resounding noise like a pistol shot that acts as a warning signal to others.

Moose are quite common in summer along the margins of the half million lakes that dot the forest. They can often be seen knee-deep in water, munching aquatic vegetation. They swim well and will dive down to the lake bed to reach succulent roots and shoots. In mid-September the forest resounds with the bawling of the cow moose enticing a mate, and the coughing bellow of the responding bull. Despite their great size, moose fall prey to wolves, especially in winter, while wolverine, cougar and bears will take the calves.

This is the realm of the lynx, which in winter stalks the snowshoe hare. In the trees the supreme nightime hunter is the marten, which can outmanoeuvre red squirrels and is equally agile on the ground pursuing chipmunks, voles and rabbits. Like other members of the weasel family, the marten has a pair of scent glands under its tail, the secretion from which is used to mark out its territory.

The great horned owl nests in the dense forest. It seldom makes its own nest, taking over the previous year's nests of hawks or crows. Egg laying and incubation take place early, well before the snow has cleared. A powerful bird, it hunts prey as large as rabbits and hares. The bird is fearless when it comes to defending its young, and bird ringers have found to their cost that when approaching they must wear protective clothing, especially hard industrial hats.

It is incredible how in early summer the deep woods become alive with the high pitched calls of warblers, which in many cases have wintered as far away as South and Central America. Each species keeps to its own particular stratum of the forest. The Cape May warbler sings from the topmost branches of the tallest spruce trees. Beneath it is the bay-breasted warbler, and in more open clearings the sombre Tennessee warbler holds sway, while in areas of secondary conifer growth lives the brightly marked Magnolia warbler, streaked black, white, yellow and grey. These warblers are extremely useful in helping to keep down the plagues of harmful defoliating insects, especially caterpillars.

Grasslands
In Canada's dry interior, south of the great forest belt, lie the grasslands – the northern extension of the prairies of the United States. Alberta's grasslands cover an extensive 30 million acres, three quarters of the area of the province. The grasslands divide into shortgrass, midgrass and tallgrass prairie according to the soil and rainfall. There are also extensive hilly areas known as rangelands. On the edge of the grassland, aspen parkland forms a buffer zone between the prairies and the forests. Here the red-eyed vireo suspends its pocket-like nest from the finer branches. The nest incorporates the paper fragments of wasp nests, mosses, lichens and plant fibres all bound

together with spiders' webs. In clearings, the ruffed grouse beats out its drumming courtship call, making a sound like the throbbing of a far off motor boat. At dusk the veery thrush calls its descending note. Medium-sized mammals: hares, woodchuck, skunks and porcupines, are common, often using each other's well-worn feeding trails.

The grasslands proper are home to Richardson's ground squirrel, detected by its piping whistle call. Its pale yellow fur blends in well with the bleached grasses and light-toned prairie soils. The animal lives in loose underground colonies and is most numerous where the soil is dry and easily worked from drought or overgrazing. The squirrel has many predators, including hawks, eagles, coyotes, and the badger, which digs them out of their burrows with its powerful, clawed front paws.

Pronghorn antelope prefer the rolling rangeland hills dotted with sagebrush and other shrubs. Pronghorn belong to a family all their own and have unusual horns that are bony extensions of the skull, covered with blackish sheaths. Pronghorn are extremely fleet footed and can reach speeds of 50 miles an hour when pursued, maintaining a steady 30 miles an hour for several miles, and great leaps of 20 feet or more are not unusual. They are restless animals, always on the move, traveling in large herds in spring and summer and smaller groups during the harsh winters, when many die from starvation.

The plains buffalo is an animal that once roamed the prairies in the millions but was nearly wiped out by the invasion of the European settlers. Today, the buffalo flourishes in national parks and sanctuaries, where its interesting behavior can be observed, including its habit of taking dust baths in the dry earth excavated by ground squirrels.

The prairies can be desolate in winter, but in spring and summer colorful flowers bloom among the grasses: the prairie crocus in the spring, the prairie sunflower in June, followed by flame-red lilies and the late summer purple flower spikes of blazing star, which grows mainly on sandy hillsides.

The Mountain Barrier

Between the prairies and the Pacific Ocean lies a great expanse of mountainous land some 400 miles (650km) wide and 1,600 miles (2600km) long extending north into the Yukon. This, the magnificent Western Cordillera, includes row upon row of mountain chains. The famous Rockies make up just one part of the eastern flank. Along the coast, where the rainfall is highest, grow dense rain forests, with stands of Sitka spruce, red cedar, hemlock and Douglas fir.

The Pacific Ocean and the rivers that feed it are rich in fish, seals, whales and seabirds. The most famous fish are the several species of salmon that migrate from the sea up the rivers to spawn. Sockeye salmon, most valued for their red, oil-rich flesh, prefer to spawn in streams that have lakes in their watershed, where the young salmon fatten up for a few years before migrating out to sea. Chum, the last salmon to spawn, may travel in the fall a few thousand miles up river in the Yukon before reaching its favoured spawning grounds.

The spawning process is a dramatic event, perfectly synchronized so that eggs and sperm are relased at the same time. All female salmon dig out their nests by making flicking movements of their sides and tail. After laying, the female covers the eggs and guards them until, too weak to maintain her post, she is carried downstream by the current to die. In most cases salmon die after spawning, their bodies providing a rich source of food for bears, gulls and especially the bald eagle, a bird that lives mainly on dead fish.

A real gem of the Pacific Coast is Queen Charlotte Island, especially its southern shore, which is rich in tidepools full of multicolored sea stars, snails, sea anemones and sea squirts. On the Kerourard Islands to the south lies the largest rookery of Stellar's sea lions on the Pacific coast. The whole coastal region is famous for its unusual seabirds such as the rhinoceros auklet and petrels that feed far out to sea and feed their young only at night on their regurgitated stomach contents.

Inland, mountain streams cut gorges through soft shale rocks. The banks of these rushing streams are the nesting place of the harlequin duck, named for the clown-like plumage of the male. When the young are ready they pop out of the nest and land right in the water, bobbing up and down like black and white balls of fluff, following their mothers over the rapids. Another bird that often nests near mountain streams is the 3.5 inch (9cm) rufous hummingbird. The nest, a tiny cup of lichens, saddles a low-sloping conifer branch that often stretches out over the water.

The gorges and canyons are criss-crossed with the trails of mountain sheep, who use them as safe transit routes and rest areas away from the attentions of the mountain lion or cougar.

In alpine clearings grow blue lupins, wild geranium and brown-eyed susan. The soil here is worked by the Columbian ground squirrels, prey of the golden eagles that build their eyries high up on rocky crags.

In southern British Columbia are dry mountain valleys with a sparse growth of sagebush and prickly pear cactus. The region is scattered with rockslides and scrub, and white jack rabbits are common. This is also the haunt of the northern Pacific rattler, which dens up during the winter months. They can often be seen in groups, sunning themselves at the den entrance in the spring sunshine.

Mixed Forests of the East

Ontario has forests reminiscent of the hardwoods of the United States, made up of basswood, white elm, ash and poplar. The wildlife here is most abundant in the marshes and wooded swamps, where spotted turtles bask on logs and herons hunt an abundance of small fish and frogs. Herons nest in colonies in trees lining the river valleys. Around the wooded wetland margins the bobcat patrols for rabbits and rodents. Here in the mixed woods is the northerly range of the Virginian opossum, a marsupial that bears up to 20 young that are nourished for up to six weeks in its pouch.

The islands around Newfoundland provide a bonanza for the birdwatcher, equivalent in many ways to those of the Pacific Coast. Here most birds nest on the rock faces, and as well as nurres, puffins and gulls, there thrive colonies of gannets that drop from heights of over 100 feet (30m) to plunge and nosedive into the sea, scattering a shoal of fish, and diving below them and snatching them before surfacing.

In these eastern latitudes of Canada lie over a third of her national parks, and one of the most popular is Point Pelee. The most southerly of them all, Point Pelee is a fiercely-protected haven for marsh birds, which can be easily observed from long boardwalks. Here too occurs the annual fall attraction of the spectacular congregation of monarch butterflies before they migrate hundreds of miles south to winter in Mexico.

Like many eastern national parks, Point Pelee lies only an hour or two from major towns and cities, and typifies the easily accessible national park that is both well facilitated and of absorbing interest. It may, of course, contrast heavily with the dramatically-scenic landscapes and imposing wildlife of the Northwest Territories – such as Wood Buffalo, with its 17,000 square miles of forest, lakes and rivers and its celebrated bison and crimson-crested whooping cranes; or Nahanni, the pure, untamed wilderness teeming with grizzlies, Dall's sheep, wolverines, nighthawks and red squirrels, accessible only by air or water, and offering the perfect opportunity for shooting the rapids by canoe through deep river canyons and past glaciers of the bluest ice.

But the contrast defends or excuses no preference. It is in essence nothing more, and nothing less, than a reflection of the enormous range of fascinating wildlife and magnificent landscapes that not only Canada's national parks, but all of Canada's vast natural and rural regions have to offer, both as part of the world ecosystem and as a contribution to the education and delight of humankind.

Facing page: a whitetail doe on the alert for the safety of her fawn.

Facing page: a wapiti or elk stag with a third-year set of antlers. These are shed in February or March, and a new set grows in April. With the arrival of heavy snows, wapiti come down off the high ground to the sheltered valleys. Top: a female wapiti with twin calves. Though a single offspring is usual, twins are not uncommon. Above: two wapiti stags browsing on grasses at the edge of the forest, and (left) a wapiti hind.

Above: cougar cubs. Young cougars stay with their mothers for up to two years. Top: a pair of older cougar cubs, showing the animals' beautiful fur color. Facing page: the cougar's hind legs are a good deal longer than its front ones. Right: a cougar yawns and shows the mark of a meat-eater – large and pointed canine teeth.

Not all black bears are black – indeed brown ones (facing page) are quite common. Top: a black bear in a swampy hollow. They need to drink frequently and are usually found near water. Above: black bears learn to climb at an early age. Left: a black bear feeding on late autumn berries. Above left: a grizzly bear, easily identifiable by its muscular shoulder hump, pads through the snow.

Previous pages: (bottom left) a magnificent bull elk with a set of 7-point antlers, (top left) a younger elk stag with newly-grown antlers, (top right) a small herd of pronghorn antelope sticking together as snow sweeps the prairies and (bottom right) a bull elk after snow. Rocky Mountain goats (left, top and facing page bottom) are expert climbers and have a fine wool undercoat covered by long, white hair. Above: mountain goat kids and (facing page top) a Dall's sheep ram and kid.

The red squirrel (facing page top and above) feeds on nuts and on the cones of pine, spruce and fir. The golden-mantled ground squirrel (top) finds its habitat in logged pine forests with rocky outcrops, while Richardson's ground squirrel (left) is a burrowing rodent of the prairies and the least chipmunk (facing page bottom) is an agile animal of forest clearings.

Eat or be eaten in the reptile world. Above left: a northern Pacific rattlesnake swallows a garter snake and (above right) a pair of raccoons investigate a bull snake they have killed. This snake is non-poisonous, though it does vibrate its tail in rattlesnake fashion. Top: a northern ribbon snake in the act of swallowing a frog. Facing page: (top) a bull snake and its prey – a deer mouse. Bull snakes are considered useful as they eat a lot of rodents. Bottom: a western blue racer about to strike a leopard frog.

The coyote (left) has a narrow chest, long legs and a slender muzzle. Top: a wolf walks stealthily through hard packed snow; its loosely-held tail shows it to be relaxed. Like dogs, wolves are unable to perspire, and pant (above) in warm weather. Facing page: (top) a wolf beside its kill in a clearing and (bottom) a watchful wolf and its prey, a young Hereford calf.

The Columbian ground squirrel (facing page) is one of the largest of the group, growing up to 16 inches (40cm) long. It excavates large and complex burrow systems, while the striped skunk (top) prefers farmland and light woodland. The fisher (left) is a fast and powerful hunter of the far north. In winter it feeds mainly on snowshoe hares, and porcupines (above).

In winter pronghorn (above, top and right) travel in mixed herds of males, females and juveniles. They feed on herbs and grasses, are extremely agile animals and are able to detect a moving object three or four miles away. Their chief enemy is the coyote, which can trap them in deep snow. Facing page: pronghorn kids follow their mothers for up to four to six weeks and then, little by little, they start to feed by themselves.

Facing page: a spawning run of kokanee, or sockeye salmon, that spend all their lives in fresh water, migrating from a lake up into feeder streams. These are fourth or fifth year fish, found in West Canada. Left: a gull on the lookout for salmon eggs and dead fish. Salmon (top and above) spawn in clear, shallow water with a gravel sand bottom. The males generally have hooked jaws.

Black bears often spend hours sitting out on the limb of a
tree (above). Facing page: (top) the black bear's long tongue is
useful in reaching beetle grubs and for lapping up ants.
(Bottom) a young black bear cautiously examining a tree
trunk.

Stellar's sea lion – or the northern sea lion (facing page) – occurs in its greatest numbers in the Gulf of Alaska. They spend most of their lives at sea, coming ashore in May to form breeding colonies, in which they stay for three months. A male Stellar sea lion (left) may weigh up to 2,200 pounds (1,000 kg). Above and top: gulls, the most common birds of the coast. Overleaf: a pair of male polar bears fight for dominance.

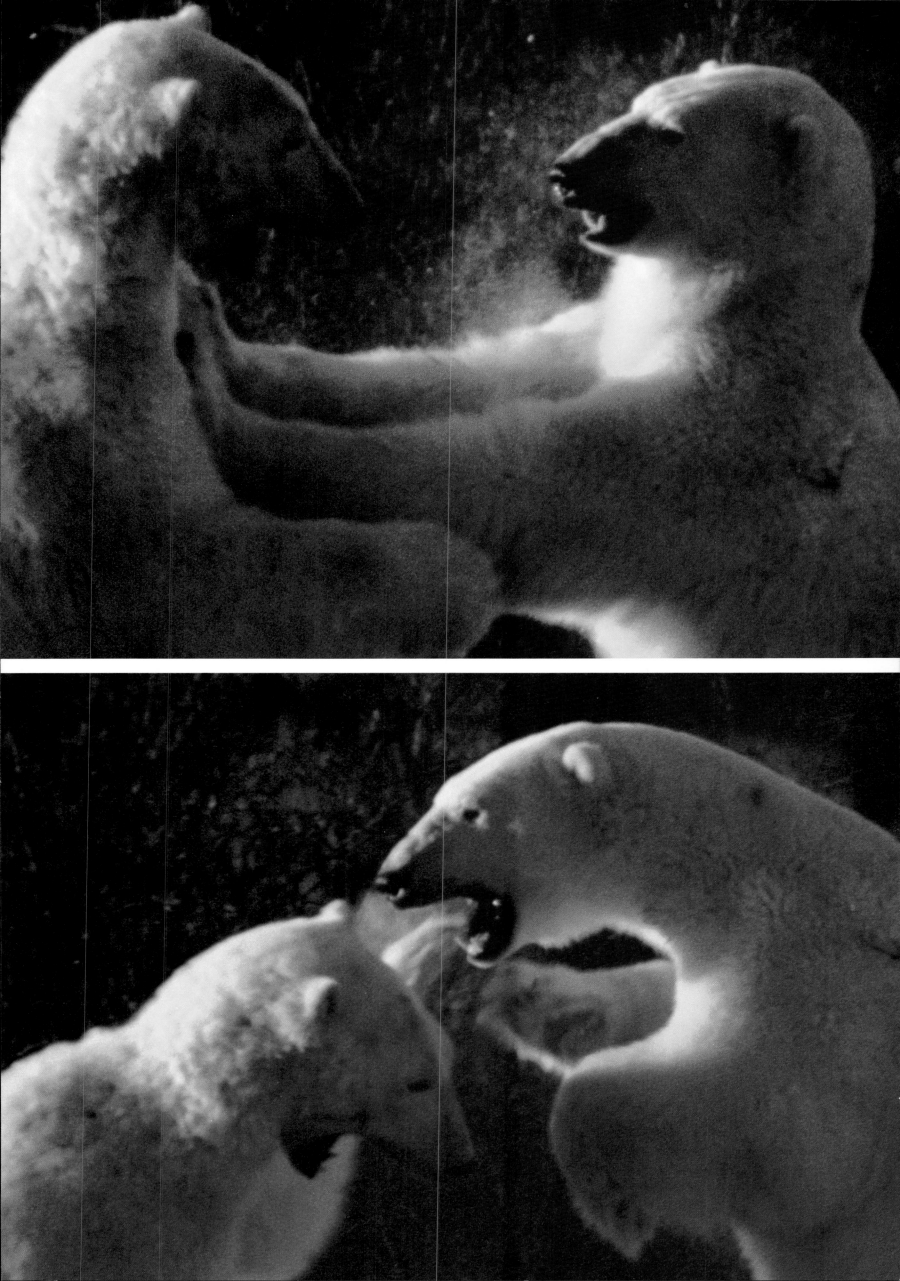

Clark's nutcracker (top) lives in open conifer woods in the west of Canada. Above: pigeons, and (above right) the emperor goose, a rare winter visitor to the coast of British Columbia. The other common name for the spruce grouse (right) is "fool hen" because it is very tame and can often be killed with a stick or stone. It prefers the forest edges and blueberry barrens. The wild turkey (facing page) was once extinct in Canada, but attempts have now been made to reintroduce it into hardwood forests.

Previous pages: a small herd of elk, led by the dominant male, heads for the shelter and security of the forest. A bull elk (facing page top) bellows out a high pitched roar or bugle, a cougar (facing page bottom), like all cats, will growl, hiss and purr, the black bear (top) can growl, squeal and grunt, while the howl of the wolf (right) is a sign of the true wilderness. Above: a bobcat snarls threateningly, exposing its sharp teeth.

Magnificent birds of prey. The powerful golden eagle (top left) makes its home in mountainous country, while the prairie falcon (right) is found in dry, open country of the west, as is Swainson's hawk (facing page top): it hunts mainly prairie dogs and gophers as well as large insects such as grasshoppers. The red-tailed hawk (top right) is a lazy hunter that soars high above the ground, and the bald eagle (facing page bottom) eats fish and also takes sick ducks and game birds. Above: marsh hawk eggs and nestlings.

Surviving winter. Facing page: (bottom) the pronghorn's coarse winter coat protects it against biting winds. Top: a cow moose and calf. During winter moose may starve as they need up to 60 pounds (27kg) of food per day. Caribou (above) can detect food under 7 inches (18cm) of snow.

Black bears (these pages) usually stand a little less than 3 feet (0.9m) at the shoulder. They will often climb trees to rest, to feed, or to escape danger, and will rub themselves against tree trunks to relieve itching.

When stalking prey, cougars (above and top) move with
extraordinary stealth. Facing page: the cougar's soft markings
blend in well with various habitats.

Facing page bottom: a bull moose shows the stump of its new antlers. When fully-grown, the adult (facing page top) may weigh up to 1,800 pounds (816kg). Top: an unusual and less than serious combat between moose and mule deer. Above: a bull moose in fresh snow.

Left: female and young black widow spiders recently hatched out from the large egg case. The black widow is dangerous and is often found near human habitation. The female is glossy black with a reddish hourglass pattern on its underside. The tiger swallowtail (top) is a common butterfly that has a strong, gliding flight and is attracted to garden flowers. Its caterpillar feeds on the leaves of various trees. Garden spiders (facing page top) were introduced to North America from Europe. They build their webs over shrubbery and between plants. Facing page bottom: a beautifully symmetrical web of one of the orb weavers, a huge family of spiders with several hundred North American species.

Above: most of Canada's musk ox population lives on the islands of the eastern Arctic. Top: the wood bison may stand as much as 7 feet (2.1m) at the shoulder. Facing page: a plains bison in a blizzard. The massive head acts as an efficient snow plough to enable the animal to get at the vegetation underneath.

Top: a cougar stretches to scratch its head on a thorn bush, showing the full extent of its long, lithe, powerful body. Males may reach 9 feet (2.8m) including the long, cylindrical tail. When cougar cubs (facing page top) are about six weeks old the mother introduces them to a meat diet.

portraits. Only elk stags support antlers. When the
lers are growing they are covered with a spongy
stance known as velvet, shed in the fall when the
lers have fully developed. An elk with six prongs to
h antler is known as a Royal Stag, with seven, an
perial Stag.

The bobcat (facing page) lives in wooded and rocky areas of southern Canada while the larger lynx (top) prefers dense northern forests. Above right: a lynx with its prey, a Californian quail. Californian bighorn sheep (above) are found in the interior of British Columbia. Right: a Rocky Mountain bighorn ram.

Above: a long-billed curlew, a breeding bird of the grasslands of southern Western Canada. The great blue heron (remaining pictures), Canada's largest heron, is a statuesque bird that spears prey with its powerful beak.

Left: in summer caribou feed on various plants but in winter they exist mainly on lichens. Moose (remaining pictures) are solitary animals that feed on a range of vegetation including water plants.

Above: a mountain bluebird at its nest hole, (top left) a killdeer on its nest, (top right) a yellow-bellied sapsucker with its beak full of insects and (right) a long-billed curlew chick. Facing page: (top left) a caliope hummingbird, (top right) Bewick's wren, (bottom right) a tree swallow and (bottom left) a yellow-headed blackbird.

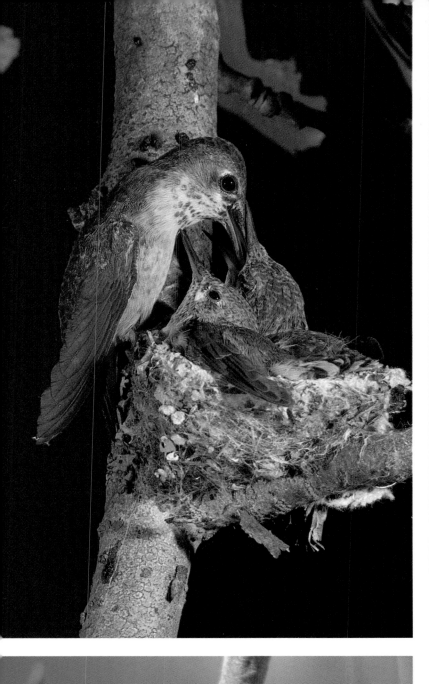

Facing page: (bottom) the American badger shows its powerful digging claws. Young opossums (facing page top) may travel on their mother's back for three months. Top: young chipmunks in a tree stump nest, (above) an adult chipmunk and (left) Richardson's ground squirrel, an alert animal of the rolling prairies.

Previous pages: Canada geese in flight. They can be distinguished from other geese by their large white cheek patches. The typical call when flying is a nasal "ka-ronk," slightly slurred at the end. Canada geese nest over a wide area and range of habitats and often build their nests near beaver lodges. The cougar (these pages) is an all-purpose hunter that can live in a variety of habitats. It is quick to defend its young and its food from intruders.

The American badger (these pages) is a night-time hunter, digging up mammals such as ground squirrels and mice from their burrows. It is well adapted to life underground, being short and flat with large claws and a well developed sense of smell.

When danger threatens, a mother black bear often sends her cubs (these pages) up the tallest tree. Black bear cubs are extremely inquisitive – sniffing, digging and investigating everything they come across, mainly to see if they can eat it. Black bears have a very mixed diet, including berries, roots, insects and small mammals. Overleaf: elk stags engage antlers in a battle of strength for dominance over a harem of females.

Junior wildlife. Above: a black bear cub sharpening its claws
on the bark of a tree, and (top) red fox kittens with eyes barely
open. Facing page: (top) young coyotes at the playful stage,
and (bottom), belying its adult nature, a lynx kitten at its
most vulnerable.

Columbian ground squirrels (facing page, top and above) build elaborate tunnel systems with a central chamber lined with soft plant seeds and grasses. From the central chamber tunnels radiate out to exit near feeding grounds. Like other ground squirrels, they carry seeds in their cheek pouches and then store them in the burrow for later consumption. In Canada, the black-tailed prairie dog (right) is found only in Grasslands National Park, Saskatchewan.

Top and facing page: in the fall a victorious and dominant stag elk advertises himself by a bellowing call known as bugling. Above: an elk stag with growing antlers covered in velvet.

Facing page: a rattlesnake about to strike – its body coiled up like a spring and the rattle at the end of its tail vibrating. Top: a bullsnake and rattler in a tug-of-war battle for a mouse. Above: a dead rattlesnake, victim of extreme cold. Right: the Pacific rattlesnake, which lives in dry, desert-like

The osprey (left and facing page bottom) is a bird of prey that builds its nest in tall trees near water. It lives almost exclusively on fish, which it snatches from or near the surface in its sharp talons. The American avocet (top and facing page top) calls an alarm-like "kleep" when disturbed. Its preferred habitat is the shallow lakes and sloughs of the southern Prairie Provinces. The herring gull (above) is a universal scavenger.

Facing page: a saw-whet owl and its prey. This 8-inch (20cm) bird prefers to nest in moist, mixed forest. The great horned owl (top and right) is Canada's largest and takes prey such as hares. Above: a male and (above right) a female snowy owl, a species that breeds in the Arctic tundra.

93

Facing page: (bottom) a cow elk in the thick of the forest, and
(top) a bull elk escorting his cows into the woods. In winter a
large bull (top) will generally separate from the cow herds to
winter apart. Above: young elk on the alert at the forest edge.

Raccoons (these pages) live in southern Canada and prefer areas with large trees, where they make dens. Young raccoons are called kits, and up to seven youngsters may be born at one time. Raccoons are generally active at night, when they go foraging for food.

The black oystercatcher (left) is a breeding bird of the rocky Pacific coast, while the chukar partridge (above left) is an Asian bird introduced to Canada. Above: a ptarmigan in summer dress and (top) a Californian quail. Facing page: (top) a wild turkey in the snow and (bottom) a ringneck pheasant.

Facing page: (top) a badger and (bottom) a red fox vixen display formidable sets of teeth. Play is important for young red foxes (top) as it teaches them to develop their hunting skills. Above: its face covered in dirt, a badger emerges after underground tunneling. Left: a bighorn ram in dominant pose.

The golden eagle (facing page) is distinguished by its strong, hooked beak, overall brown plumage and feathered legs. Its favorite hunting grounds are foothills with grassy pastures where prey such as the yellow-bellied marmot live. Remaining pictures: an eagle with its marmot prey.

Bighorn rams (previous pages) isolate themselves from the herds of females and young for much of the year. Rams weigh on average 250 pounds (114kg). These pages: cougar youngsters play and fight together like the young of many carnivorous mammals. Hunting involves tracking the prey through very many different types of habitat.

Rocky mountain rams spend a lot of time fighting with each other either for dominance within the all male herd or, during the winter rutting period, when they clash horns to win the females. Large horns weigh up to 35 pounds (16kg).

Canada geese (these pages) prefer to nest in the muskeg region of the Hudson Bay lowlands, a largely waterlogged plain. A pair with the young of that year are inseparable. The female leads the way, followed by the young, with the gander bringing up the rear. The young fly south with their parents in the fall and do not separate from them until they return the following spring to the nesting grounds.

Above: an elk calf with its typical, spotted coat, born in late May or early June. Facing page: mountain caribou (top) give birth to their fawns in mid-June, in hilly terrain. Bottom: plains buffalo calves are a bright reddish tan when newly born.

Top: a black bear eyes proceedings warily, while (facing page)
a grizzled specimen does the same from a bed of horsetail
plants. Above: a sow black bear and her yearling cub
investigate a deer carcass.

The Canada goose (these pages) is **the** wild goose of the country. Most people see it on its spring or fall migration to and from its breeding grounds. Its nest is a depression in the ground lined with sticks and dried stems, with an inner lining of down. The young hatch out after 28 to 33 days.

Left: a whitetail deer buck. Making its home, for preference, at the edges of hardwood forests, this is probably the most widespread game animal of North America. Top: a mule deer buck and (above) a doe mule deer, in deep snow. Facing page: (top) mule deer bucks in rut, and (bottom) young mule deer bucks, their breath making clouds of vapor in the cold air.

Facing page: in Canada, the white-footed mouse (top) is uncommon and is found only in dry, eastern deciduous forests. The yellow-bellied marmot (bottom) is a sociable animal of rocky hillsides. The badger (top) eats a wide range of animal food including snakes. The pika (above left) is a small, stocky, tailless animal rather like a guinea pig and lives above the treeline in the Rocky Mountains. The hoary marmot (above right) likes areas strewn with large boulders.

The mobile and sensitive lips of the black bear (above) help when the animal feeds on small items such as plant shoots or berries. Facing page: black bears climb by a series of quick bounds, grasping with their forepaws and pushing with their hind legs.

The mountain goat's beautiful winter coat (facing page, above and above right) is long and silky and its undercoat finer than cashmere. The fleece was used by the Indians of the Pacific coast to weave the famous Chilkat blankets. Between the end of May and mid-July the winter coat is shed in patches, resulting in a straggly, unkempt appearance (top). Right: a Rocky Mountain sheep bighorn ram.

Clark's nutcracker (top and facing page) feeds on nuts and conifer seeds. Above: a male mountain bluebird at its nest in an abandoned woodpecker hole, (above right) the gray jay of the northern forests, and (right) Stellar's jay, which lives in western Canada. Overleaf: the Pacific rattlesnake, (top left) at a den entrance, (bottom left) mating and (top right) swallowing a mouse. Bottom right: a snake's tongue acts as an extremely effective sense organ.

The bobcat (facing page) is not hunted a great deal for its fur, which is soft and not very durable. The lynx (this page) molts its long guard hairs in the spring and in the fall. Overleaf: Canadian canids. The Arctic fox (bottom left) has a very keen sense of smell, while the coyote (top left) is an intelligent animal, very wary of man. Top right: Northern timberline wolves and (bottom right) a red fox.

The painted turtle (top) is common in weedy ponds and lakes and can often be seen sunning itself on a log. The western spotted frog (right) spends most of the summer in and around water. Above: a tussock moth caterpillar crawls up a log invaded by slime mold fungus, while (facing page) a bumblebee searches for nectar on the flowerhead of a member of the thistle family.

A wealth of wildfowl. The green-winged teal (left), Canada's smallest duck, measures 14.5 inches (36cm). Above left: the male greater scaup, (top) American coots displaying, and (above) the common loon, which returns to its breeding grounds soon after the winter ice breaks up. Facing page: (top) a wood duck and (bottom) a mallard hen and ducklings.

Top, left and above: different color phases of the black bear. Facing page: (top) a sow black bear with twin cubs. Black bear cubs (facing page bottom) spend over a year with their mother before she mates again.

The bighorn sheep (above left) gives birth to its young in late May or early June. The white-tailed deer doe (above right, top and facing page top) usually bears a single fawn after its first pregnancy. The fawn can stand within a few hours. Facing page bottom: pronghorns in the snow.

A distinctive feature of the golden eagle (facing page and above left) is the yellow, fleshy cere at the base of the bill, which is nearly as long as the bird's head. Top: a red-tailed hawk mantling its prey, (left) a fledgling red-tailed hawk and (above) a goshawk, a bird of forest edges and clearings.

The nutria or coypu (above) is from South America and was introduced into Canada and North America for its fine fur. The beaver (top) is a large rodent that weighs up to 60 pounds (27kg). Muskrats (facing page) live in wetlands and build domed houses.

A young elk (left) will be large at birth and may weigh up to 45 pounds (20kg). A mule deer fawn (above) remains in one place for a month before following its mother to feed. Facing page: (top) a white-tailed deer doe and fawn and (bottom) mule deer twins, a usual occurance. Overleaf: (bottom left) a coyote on the alert and (top left) coyotes on moose kill. (Top right) a timber wolf relaxing in the sun and (bottom right) a red fox at the entrance to its den, often an abandoned woodchuck burrow.

The European mute swan (top) is an introduced species and has become wild in a few parts of Canada. The whistling swan (above), a magnificent, all-white bird, breeds in the Canadian low Arctic. Left: a coot feeding its young and (above left) a red-winged blackbird and swan. Facing page: snow geese (top) can be seen in large numbers in the fall at Cap Tourmente, east of Quebec City. (Bottom) a mallard hen with nestlings.

Despite its enormous beak, the bald eagle (these pages) is more of a scavenger than an active hunter. It eats mainly dead fish washed up on the coast, or by lakes and rivers. It has declined in numbers, and is more common on the Pacific coast. Its nest, built in a tall tree, may become huge as it is often returned to year after year.

Elk portraits. Top: combats between elk stags include shoving with their antlers, which seldom lock as do those of moose, caribou and deer. They also lash at each other with their forefeet, rising up high on their hind legs. Facing page bottom: a victorious bull.

Facing page: a mule deer buck. During the summer the bucks live in high alpine meadows. Antlers are carried only by the male and are shed in the spring. Top: a mule deer doe and fawn and (left) a doe mule deer with a grizzled, brown winter coat. In winter, mule deer travel in mixed herds led by an experienced doe. The rut of the whitetail deer (above) starts in mid October and continues until late December.

Cougars (these pages) hunt mainly at night. Their favorite prey is deer, which they kill by leaping on their backs and biting deep at the base of the neck. The carcass is usually dragged off to a safe eating place. Cougars sometimes raid farms to take domestic stock. A mother bison (overleaf) will charge an intruder in defence of her young calf.